MY NEW PET

MY PET RABBIT

BY NANCY GREENWOOD

Gareth Stevens PUBLISHING

Please visit our website, www.garethstevens.com. For a free color catalog of all our high-quality books, call toll free 1-800-542-2595 or fax 1-877-542-2596.

Portions of this work were originally authored by Cecelia H. Brannon and published as *Pet Rabbits*. All new material this edition authored by Nancy Greenwood.

Library of Congress Cataloging-in-Publication Data
Names: Greenwood, Nancy, author.
Title: My pet rabbit/ Nancy Greenwood.
Description: New York : Gareth Stevens Publishing, [2023] | Series: My new pet | Includes index.
Identifiers: LCCN 2022000145 (print) | LCCN 2022000146 (ebook) | ISBN 9781538281123 (set) | ISBN 9781538281130 (library binding) | ISBN 9781538281116 (paperback) | ISBN 9781538281147 (ebook)
Subjects: LCSH: Rabbits–Juvenile literature.
Classification: LCC SF453.2 .G74 2023 (print) | LCC SF453.2 (ebook) | DDC 636.935–dc23/eng/20220111
LC record available at https://lccn.loc.gov/2022000145
LC ebook record available at https://lccn.loc.gov/2022000146

Published in 2023 by
Gareth Stevens Publishing
29 East 21st Street
New York, NY 10010

Designer: Andrea Davison-Bartolotta
Editor: Kristen Nelson

Photo credits: Cover, p. 1 Dagmar Hijmans/Shutterstock.com; series art (interior backgrounds) Magnia/Shutterstock.com; p. 5 Krakenimages.com/Shutterstock.com; p. 7 Elizabett/Shutterstock.com; p. 9 (top left) Flying broccoli/Shutterstock.com; p. 9 (top right) Sofiya Stoyakina/Shutterstock.com; p. 9 (bottom left) Regien Paassen/Shutterstock.com; p. 9 (bottom right) Cora Mueller/Shutterstock.com; p. 11 Farhad Ibrahimzade/Shutterstock.com; p. 13 BIGANDT.COM/Shutterstock.com; p. 15 Boban Vaiagich/Shutterstock.com; p. 17 ARTFULLY PHOTOGRAPHER/Shutterstock.com; p. 19 Yuliya Machulan/Shutterstock.com; p. 21 BearFotos/Shutterstock.com.

Printed in the United States of America

CONTENTS

Boldface words appear in the glossary.

Get a Rabbit?

What's cuter than a fluffy rabbit? These **popular** pets are found in many homes. But, before getting a rabbit, you need to know how much care they may need! It can be a big **responsibility**.

Know What To Do

There are many kinds of rabbits. However, they're all somewhat nervous animals. Rabbits aren't great pets for very small children. They need to be handled with a **gentle** touch. Talking to a rabbit softly can help make it feel better.

Cuddly Look

Rabbits have long, soft ears. Some rabbits have ears that stand up. Other rabbits have ears that hang down. Rabbits have very soft fur. Rabbits come in many colors. They can be brown, black, gray, or white. Some are more than one color.

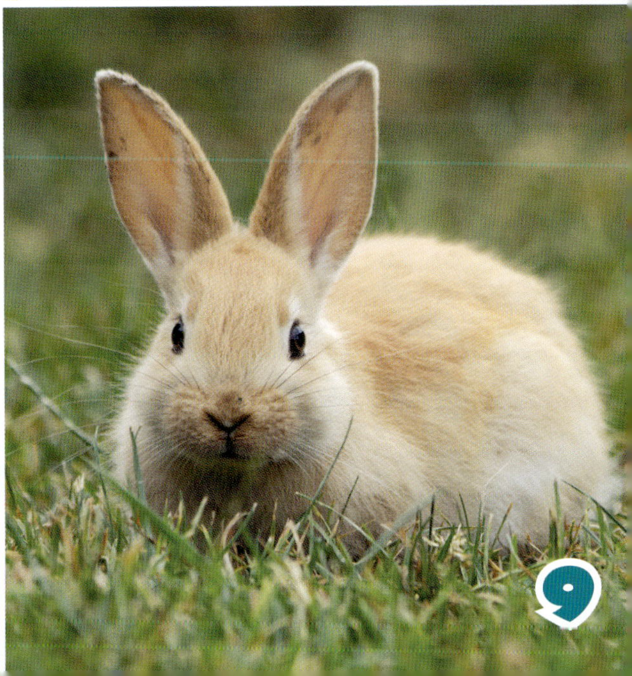

Hutch Life

Pet rabbits are often kept in cages. You need to make sure that the cage for your rabbit is large enough. Sometimes, a rabbit's cage or area has a **hutch**. All rabbit living areas should be cleaned at least every other day.

Caring for Rabbits

Rabbits are **herbivores**. They need to eat fruits, vegetables, and special hay to stay healthy. They also need **pellets** made for rabbits. Rabbits eat a little bit many times a day. All that chewing helps keep their teeth short. Rabbits need fresh water too.

Yearly visits to the vet, or animal doctor, keep your rabbit healthy. Rabbits need **grooming** too. Brush your rabbit a few times a week. Some rabbits have longer fur and may need extra brushing. Rabbits need their nails clipped too.

Make part of your house safe for your rabbit. Pet rabbits need to be let out of their cage every day to play and exercise. You can have a safe place for them to go outside when the weather is good too!

Stay Social

Rabbits like to live in groups. So, if you only have one rabbit, you need to **socialize** with your rabbit often. Some rabbits are shy and may need very gentle handling. These animals are most active in the morning and evening. That's when to play!

Long Life

When treated well, pet rabbits can live to be more than 10 years old! That's a big **commitment**. Take time to learn more about rabbits and talk to your family. Then, decide whether a pet rabbit it right for you!

GLOSSARY

commitment: A promise to do something.

gentle: Having a kind and quiet nature.

grooming: The process of cleaning the fur, skin, or feathers.

herbivore: An animal that only eats plants.

pellet: A small, hard ball of food.

popular: Liked by many people.

responsibility: Something a person is in charge of.

socialize: To do things with others in a friendly way.

FOR MORE INFORMATION

BOOKS

Kelly, Erin Suzanne. *Pets.* New York, NY: Children's Press, in imprint of Scholastic, Inc., 2021.

Salzmann, Mary Elizabeth. *Rabbits Are Fun!.* Minneapolis, MN: Sandcastle, an imprint of Abdo Publishing, 2022.

WEBSITES

Fun Rabbit Facts for Kids
easyscienceforkids.com/all-about-rabbits/
Check out lots of fun facts about rabbits!

10 Hopping Fun Rabbit Facts
www.natgeokids.com/uk/discover/animals/general-animals/10-hopping-fun-rabbit-facts/
Read more about rabbits and other animals here.

Publisher's note to educators and parents: Our editors have carefully reviewed these websites to ensure that they are suitable for students. Many websites change frequently, however, and we cannot guarantee that a site's future contents will continue to meet our high standards of quality and educational value. Be advised that students should be closely supervised whenever they access the internet.

INDEX